Say No to Plastic Straws

Plastic straws

This is a **plastic** straw.

3

Plastic straws
are not good
for the **environment**.

Plastic straws will stay in the environment for a long, long time.

Compost bin

The old plastic straws can not go in here.

Recycle bin

We can not put
the old plastic straws
in here.

On the beach

Look at the plastic straws.

They will stay on the sand for a long, long time.

In the ocean

Can you see
the plastic straws?

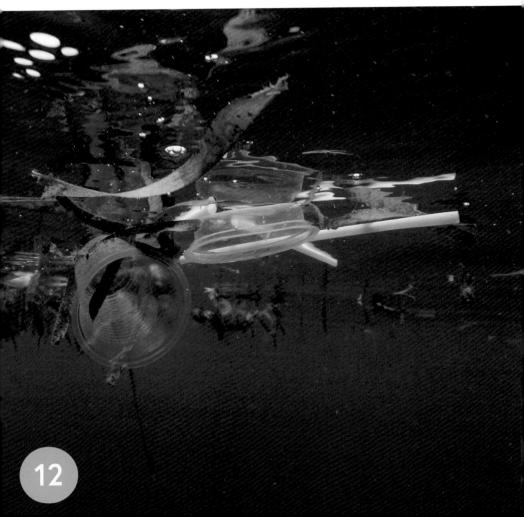

They will stay in the water for a long, long time.

No plastic straws

I will say no
to plastic straws.

15

Glossary

 environment

 plastic